Sasquatch

The Living Legend

Akanneesha

Original Art by
Alexa Evans

By

Thom Cantrall

Copyright Page

ISBN-13:

978-1479307616

Sasquatch The Living Legend
Copyright 2012 Thom Cantrall
All Rights Reserved

International copyright protection is reserved under Universal Copyright Convention and bilateral copyright relations of the USA. All rights reserved, which includes the right to reproduce this book or any portions thereof in any form whatsoever except as provided by relevant copyright laws.

Published by Createspace Inc.   www.createspace.com

Printed in USA

ISBN-13: 978-1479307616

Cover art by: Alexa Evans
Alex_art1011@Hotmail.com

Table of Contents

Proof of Sasquatch	1
Foreword	4
Proving Sasquatch	11
Introduction	12
Patterson-Gimlin Film	17
Muscle Bulge	20
Size & Gait	21
Costuming	27
Intermembral Index	35
Know Your Players	38
Conclusions on PGF	40
Footprints	43
An Observation	50
DNA Evidence	52
DNA Conclusions	59
Conclusions:	59

Foreword

In August of 1958 a road building crew working on a contract for the United States Department of Agriculture, Forest Service in the Bluff Creek area of Humboldt County, California returned to work one morning and found some very strange "calling cards" left for them. In the loose dust of the newly turned earth were  tracks of a human appearing nature. The trackway descended a very steep hillside, passed around some heavy equipment and then disappeared. The operator of one of the Caterpillar Tractors involved, Jerry Crew, photographed the discovery, made plaster casts of the tracks and called in Andrew  Genzoli, editor of the nearby Eureka, California newspaper who wrote a very compelling article that introduced the term "bigfoot" to the world.

Subsequently, several articles

on the subject were penned by renowned Zoologist, Ivan T. Sanderson. It was these articles that appeared in the magazines, "Argosy" and "True" that inspired a tall, spare fifteen year old young man to kindle an interest in a subject that has led him across the continent in its pursuit.

Dr. Sanderson brought legitimacy to a subject that was ridiculed and dismissed by almost all who heard of the incident in that northern county… all except the father of a certain fifteen year old who simply piqued his curiosity with clever queries and myriad "what if" questions. We had a family friend from the Eureka area, a sliver picker (loggers term for a sawmill worker) by the name of Everett who tried to explain that this was the track of a deranged Indian fellow who ran those hills indiscriminately. By this time Dr. Sanderson's article had appeared in "True" magazine (this article can be seen in full at

www.bigfootencounters.com/articles/true1958.htm   ) and in "Argosy" magazine. Because this had provided a forewarning and information from an expert in the field, these attempts at denial fell on deaf ears.

Dr. Sanderson has also penned many books and was the premier author on the subject of unknown animals. He was the author of the word "Cryptozoology". As can be imagined, this fifteen year old was fascinated by the subject. A fire had been ignited that burns as brightly today as it did as a sophomore at Sonoma Valley High School.

There are several major differences in that youth and the man who pens this today... I no longer have to wonder if this being exists. I no longer read of the exploits of others and wish me there. I have met these magnificent beings and they me. I have sojourned with them. I understand them and I learn from them. I have written of them and continue to do so today.

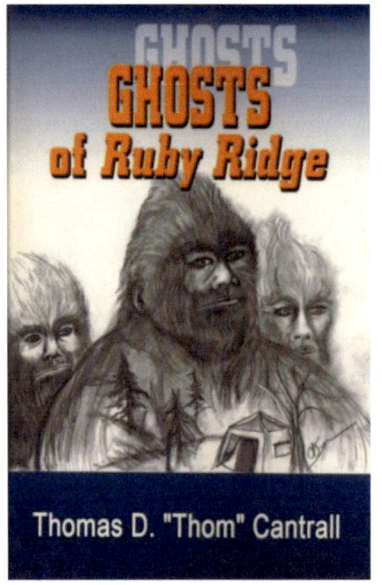

For more than thirty five years I would tell no one of what I was seeing or the reactions I was getting. My father was gone, so I had no confidant. The rest of my family did not share my ardor or my understanding, so, I simply kept what I knew to myself. That changed in 2009 when I published my first book, "Ghosts of Ruby Ridge" (www.ghostsofrubyridge.com).

The change began with the end of the 20th Century when I asked myself why I cared what other people thought. How did I know they did think? In fact, it has been made known to me that very few actually do. All they do is parrot what others, probably unthinking themselves, have said. I realize that what I know to be true, I alone know. No one was with me when I had the experiences that formulated my life in this field so how could anyone know exactly what I knew? Of course there were others who had similar experiences, but they were just that, similar. They were not my experiences.

RESPECT PROTECT

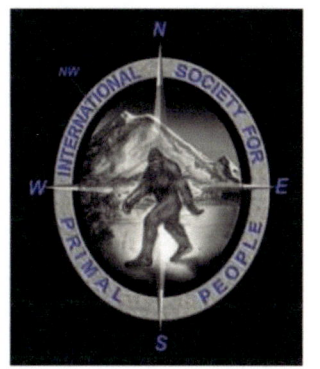

Homo sapiens hirsutii

Charged with this newfound revelation, I set out to write the book. It did not take me long to complete it and I was most pleased when I had artwork done for the cover by a professional artist to see the beauty of the finished project... well... almost finished. I had to find a publisher. I learned first hand the brutality of the publishing world. I had a completed manuscript telling a compelling story but no name as a book author. Oh, I had published a ton of magazine articles dating all the way back to my sophomore year of college, but no books... I persevered, however, and it came to light. I began attending conferences and even joined the social network, Facebook to expand my contact with this subject. Two months ago I hosted the largest and one of the finest conferences on the subject of Sasquatch or bigfoot that I have ever seen or attended. Fifteen presenters from across the country assembled in my community and told an avid and excited audience exactly how it was in this world.

This book was born of that effort. Since I have been involved in this field of endeavor, there have been those who will deny and deride what others have encountered. They do so without preamble or knowledge. They simply make statements, often from things they've heard from others without any knowledge of the source of that statement and certainly without knowledge of the true facts surrounding their diatribe.

One of the favorite subjects of these people is the famed Patterson-Gimlin Film of 1967. Another is the video done by Paul Freeman in the Blue Mountains of Washington state in 1994. These are called "controversial" because people insist on making outlandish, out of context statements about them. Trust me; if you examine the FACTS of these films, there is no controversy. This book does just that. In it we will examine the statements made by PROFESSIONAL people, experts in their field as it pertains to Sasquatch. This treatise does not accept the word of the unknowing but only of those who have paid the price to be listened to and heeded.

We present this in a format wherein if one has a skeptical friend or acquaintance, he can simply hand them this small reference and tell them to, "when you learn to read, read it and learn. In the meantime there are lots of pictures for you to look at."

In short, it presents the case for the veracity of Sasquatch in the opinions, ideas, research and conclusions of those who know, not those who guess and make it up as they go.

Enjoy!

Thom

Proving Sasquatch

The Testimony of the Experts

Chapter I
Introduction

It must be made clear from the outset; no one can PROVE anything as far as these beings are concerned. Anything anywhere can be argued and refuted either in good faith or maliciously. It can be done truthfully or mendaciously depending on the individual and his end purposes. All we can do is offer evidence. Any statement made, picture displayed, video shown or audio heard serves one purpose only… it offers evidence to support the claims made by the person sharing the fact. Of course, the clearer the statement, the more esteemed the author or the more credible the subject, the stronger the evidence is.

When a discussion begins and statements are made, demand that any statement made as a representation of fact be substantiated by a reference to the person making that statement. Believe me when I say that in a court of law, "everybody knows…" or "my buddy says…" is NOT going to be allowed, nor should it be allowed here. The corollary of that is also true in that I must be prepared to support my own assertions.

All too often, the skeptic does not care about the source or the veracity of the author of the statements he repeats, therefore, it is essential that this fact be made known up front. Do not allow such statements to be considered and let the individual know that this is not acceptable in this venue.

If personal opinion is expressed, make sure it is clear that it is opinion and then determine how that speaker is qualified to make such a statement. Does he have research time in the field? Has he spent hours in the field investigating the subject at hand? Where did he come by this experience? Is he trained in this field? Does he understand the natural world in the area in which he is offering his opinion? What is the sum of his personal experiences as pertains to this statement? In the realm of personal opinion, it is essential to know how much research time does he have on the subject

Photo property of the author

under question. Exactly what are his personal experiences and where were they that would make them appropriate to this discussion.

As an example, one of the things I often discuss is the question of the amount of oxygen generated by trees. I can find a plethora of people with opinions but very few are foresters, agronomists, dendrologists botanists or even forest ecologists. They have no shortage of opinion on the subject, but few have the technical expertise or scientific training to even begin to understand the ecology of the forest biome.

It is absolutely essential to understand that argument is totally useless with these people. First, in all cases, when the voice rises, reason departs. One can only discuss these facts with reasonable, logical, open people. To do otherwise flies in the face of reality. When confronted with such a situation, merely state that you do not have time for spurious argument but if your antagonist would wish to speak from factual statements not hearsay and innuendo, you're willing to accommodate them. Remember

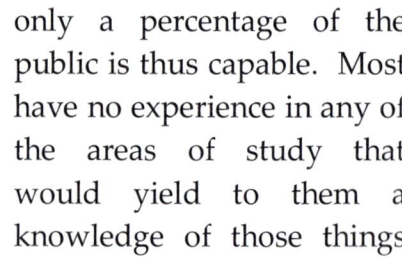

only a percentage of the public is thus capable. Most have no experience in any of the areas of study that would yield to them a knowledge of those things

14

we discuss.

Shouting matches avail nothing. There is an old adage that states that a man convinced against his will is of the same opinion still. This is especially appropriate to this discussion. One cannot overwhelm another with a preponderance of evidence or the strength of voice if the facts are not salient, appropriate and calmly presented. Even then, most often, the opponent will not admit that his stance was wrong and the best we can hope for is that he will, in his own time, review the facts presented in the context of this argument and will realize they have merit. He might then begin to adjust his thinking on the matter.

I find people in the legal profession to be the most difficult to deal with in this way. To them, lies are a way of life... they are the commonplace and the ordinary. If they have been in this field for any length of time, they are no longer capable of recognizing truth from a lie and will not

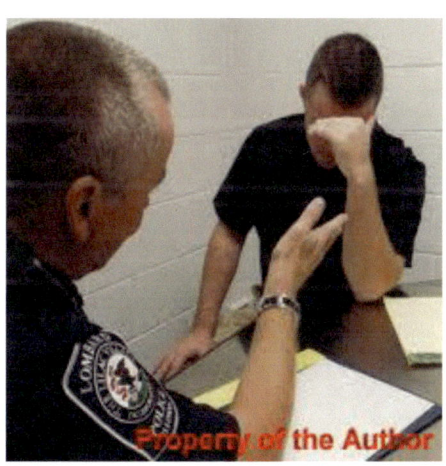

even try. If an item goes against the logic of his position, he will simply reject it out of hand. When dealing with these people and with others of their ilk, it is best to merely present one's case and close your argument. Cite your references and leave no statement without reference. To do this will go far towards making a good presentation to these people. Do not undertake to argue them into submission. Believe me, they have heard every lie ever known to mankind and are experts in spouting them back. Be very strict in requiring references for any allegation they should make.

Chapter II
The Patterson-Gimlin Film

In October of 1967, two Washington state cowboys, investigating claims of Sasquatch activity and hoping to make a documentary movie were riding on Bluff Creek in far northern California. The two men, on horseback, came around an obstacle and found themselves looking at the subject of their quest. The being who was destined to be known to the world simply as Patty was introduced to society.

Used with permission

Roger Patterson was on a young, roughly broke horse who literally exploded at the vision before him. In the midst of this bedlam, the man had to retrieve his camera from his saddlebags. While attempting to do so, the horse fell and it was necessary to avoid slashing hooves to make that retrieval. When, finally, Roger claimed his camera and moved to begin filming, he crossed Bluff Creek and fell flat on his face coming out of the creek. He quickly regained his footing and moved up onto the flat alongside the stream and began filming...

"Cover me, Bob!" he said to his partner.

Bob then removed his rifle from his saddle scabbard and watched to make sure that the large being did not attempt to attack the dismounted cameraman. "There was never any thought in my mind to shoot that creature," Bob told me face to face. "I was there only to protect Roger's life and I would have fired my rifle only to do that."

As the being moved away slowly, Roger changed position to gain a better angle and Bob rode his horse across the creek to keep them both in view.

It was at this point, frame 352 in the film, where Patty turns and looks back at the camera. She looked directly at Bob who still sat his horse with his rifle comfortably held across his saddle bows. Aware of her safety, the magnificent lady then turned back to her line of travel and proceeded on across the flat and out of the frame and into our hearts forever.

"How did it look?" a curious Bob Gimlin asked.

"I don't know, Bob, I don't know if I have anything at all. I have run out of film and I don't know if anything will show," a worried Roger answered.

What followed in the nearly half century to follow this momentous day has been an epic in incredulity. Expert after expert has testified to the veracity of the many aspects of this film. They have been largely ignored in favor of the statements of people who have no idea of what took place that day so long ago. Many people have even come forth to say that they were the subject in the suit… even though most could not identify were Bluff Creek even was, let alone how it could have been done.

Understand, there is no controversy among the experts who examined the evidence first hand at the time of discovery. The controversy comes from the statements of people who have no idea of which they speak and have no credentials to support their claims. Those who know the least are often those who speak the loudest.

With this in mind, this book is dedicated to the testimony of qualified experts. All statements herein contained are cited by name and credential. Now, to the facts…

Muscle Bulge:

Very early on in the Patterson-Gimlin Film, at Frame 5, an anomaly shows up on the right upper leg of the subject of the film. 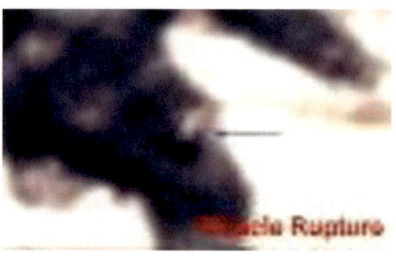 Very evident in the frame, there is a bulge in the quadriceps muscle. This is not a gunshot wound as some have purported nor is it something someone would design into a suit being built for the purpose of a hoax.

Dr. Andrew Nelson of the Center for Motion Analysis and Biomechanics stated: "This is probably a rupture of the Quadriceps Muscle… this is something that cannot be copied in a suit."

He continued, "After analyzing the biomechanical issues, I find it very hard to believe somebody in 1967 could have fabricated the intricacies as evidenced by the soft tissue irregularities seen on the upper leg. The science at that time was just far to primitive."

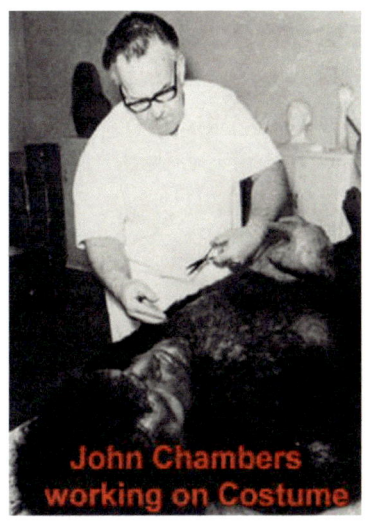

John Chambers working on Costume

John Chambers, now deceased, who won the Academy Award for costume design in 1969 for the 1968 award winning movie, "Planet of the Apes" stated: "If this is a suit, it is the finest ever devised for it was beyond our capability in the 1960s. Every hair would have had to have been individually attached to the model for this to do what it does in that film."

My question is very simple... Having heard what the experts in the field have said about this apparent rupture, does this sound like something that could have been accomplished in the remote wilds of northern California by two rodeo rough stock riders with no costuming or theatrical experience on a suit made of the hide of a red horse, as suggested by one fake Patty?

Size and Gait:

Professor Jeff Meldrum, Paleontologist, Idaho State University stated that in primates the normal ratio of foot size to height is 6.5... that the foot is generally 15.5% of the height of the individual. It should be remembered that this is a "rule of thumb" only. There will be individuals who will not conform to this standard. That said, it should be noted that the general rule will still apply.

Bob Gimlin with cast of Patty's track... property of the author

When Patty strode across that Bluff Creek sandbar, she left a very nicely defined trackway. Her prints were vivid and distinct, allowing the principles to cast the impressions using plaster of Paris as a medium. Several noted authorities were called in to verify, independently, the scene. The measured size of the track as independently corroborated by John Green, Newspaperman from British Columbia, Canada, Bob Titmus from Redding, California and Al Hodgson of Willow Creek, California, all of whom saw and measured the tracks independently was 14.5 inches.

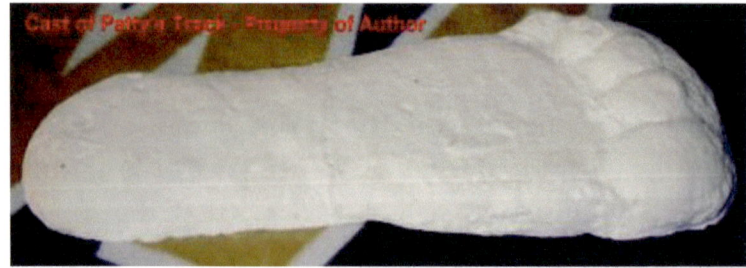

Cast of Patty's Track - Property of Author

If we use the foot length as measured by independent sources, and apply it to Dr. Meldrum's formula we get a nominal height of nearly eight feet as follows:

14.5" Track X 6.5 = 94" = 7'10" in Height

Bill Munns, Graphic Artist, Hollywood set designer and analyst took a different approach to achieve a projected height for Patty. He had the Lens and Camera data and knowing the focal length of the lens, the magnification factor of that lens and the distance from the camera to the subject, he could ascertain the height of the subject of the film.

There was some confusion initially over what lens on the triple lens camera was actually used, but computations quickly solved that anomaly and Mr. Munns was able to state quite confidently that the being in the film was between 7.5 feet and 8 feet tall as calculated.

The third method used to determine height utilizes the scene projected in Frame 72 of the film.

We know that the length of the foot shown is 14.5 inches from the measurement of the tracks. If we allow for the shoulder slump, the bowed head and the knee bend of the right leg, and the fact that the right foot is sunken into the soil a finite distance, we can approximate her height by merely comparing the length of the foot as shown in the frame. I used a pair of dividers to apply the length of the foot to her over all height and came up with a height of 7 feet 2 inches plus or minus 3 inches, or a ratio of about 6.1 times the foot length. That is certainly within the range to be expected from Dr. Meldrum's formula.

In this exercise we have used three different and distinct measuring techniques from three different experts to arrive at the same general conclusion: the subject in the film stood between 7 feet 4 inches and 7 feet 10 inches. In no case did this study yield a figure that could be construed as the height of a normal human being found in society in 1967.

Gait:

The next area of study this treatise on height leads us is to the unique gait exhibited by Patty in the film. In order to shed some light on this area of interest, we must borrow from the world of make believe again and marry that to the world of science.

Reuben Steindorf, Senior Animator at "Vision Realm, Inc.", using a system known as "Inverse Kinematics and Motion Analysis" created a 3D model of the subject in the Patterson-Gimlin film. This model was then forwarded to Dr. Andrew Nelson of the Center for Motion

Joe Russo
Used by permission

Dynamics and Biomechanics who graphically inserted a skeleton into the model of the creature.

Dr. Nelson ran an entire spectrum of tests on the test subject and determined that Patty walked with a "Compliant Gait". We humans, on the other hand, use a very stiff-legged gait in which we, essentially, pole vault over our leg and land with a very heavy heel strike. Motion Capture analysis shows that the Compliant Gait results in a very smooth, swinging stride with virtually no heel strike and very flat-footed placement of the foot on the down step.

Dr. Scott Lind and Emmy Award winning animator Joe Russo then attempted to train an athlete to walk with this same compliant gait and found that the human body was not capable of exactly duplicating this movement. They were unsuccessful in their attempts to train even an athlete to walk with this gait.

This failure caused these professional men to conclude that it **was impossible for a human to**

exactly duplicate the walking motion of the being in the Patterson-Gimlin Film.

Costuming:

An effort was made to analyze the possibility of the use of a costume in this short film. To this end, Peter Brooke, Costume Designer for the "Jim Henson Creature Shop" and famed Hollywood Costumer, John Chambers whose efforts on the "Planet of the Apes" took four professional designers three months to create, performed this examination and a thorough analysis of the being in the Patterson-Gimlin Film. These consummate

professionals concluded that there are three notable features in the film that needed to be closely examined and on which the conclusion depended. These three factors are:

Arm Length

Firm Musculature beneath the surface

The Hair Adheres to the body

 beneath it

We shall examine each of these points individually as we continue in our quest for the real facts as pertains to this film. It seems that all who I have ever heard denouncing this as a person in a suit do not know the facts that these experts have presented in their analysis.

Peter Brooke after his examinations stated unequivocally, "Such Costumes did not exist in the 1960s." The fur adheres to the form and contours of the body. Today we make such suits of four way stretch fur fabric but that did not exist until the 1980s. The era of that film did not have fur that could be form fitted."

John Chambers added to Mr. Brooke's conclusions, "It does stretch. I don't know how they could have done that in 1967. There are several individual muscle groups that are plainly visible on the creature in the film." There is even "tightening and slacking of the Achilles Tendon evident" as she walks.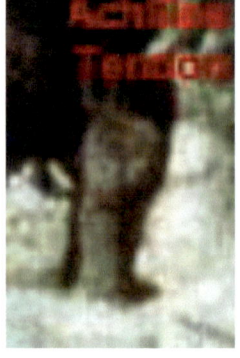

Mr. Chambers continued, stating that the "Shoulder blade is clearly visible and moves during the walk and the look back."

I believe that if I stopped here and ventured no further there could be few who could argue successfully that this film could in any way be contrived or faked. All of the factors mentioned to this point are patently visible and are easily seen by even the most ardent of skeptics... whether those skeptics would admit to seeing these factors is entirely another question and for that reason, if no other, we will go on with our treatise.

Bill Munns, Graphic Artist and Designer most noted, probably, for his large sized artistic representation of the ancient hominid, Gigantopithecus blackii, Mister  Munns has completed an thorough analysis of the requirements of a person wearing a suit such as one shown in the Patterson-Gimlin film would have to be. He was also completed an involved diagnosis of that film. I would recommend that anyone interested in this subject visit his website at www.themunnsreport.com and his series of Youtube videos at: http://www.youtube.com/watch?feature=player_embedded&v=cJZTLWUJh-w#! This is the first of a series of videos he has created concerning this subject. A treatise on the comparative anatomical features of a female model and the image of Patty is shown clearly in the video at: http://www.youtube.com/watch?v=V9WO8c38cRo&feature=relmfu

In this work, Bill Munns carefully illustrates the motions of the person doing the filming and the subject of the film as they move through the setting of the encounter. He carefully illustrates the relative positions of both entities during this time frame. Part Two illustrates the trackway and the individual tracks therein. Part Three is the most important for our purposes. In this segment, Mr. Munns analyzes the subject in the film, Patty, and compares that to an actual female subject.

In Bill Munns's characterization, he points out numerous anomalies. He illustrates with side by side comparisons the impossibility of creating any suit like that which would have necessarily have to have been used in making the Patterson-Gimlin Film. His comparisons illustrate many incompatibilities inherent with placing a human into the anatomy of the subject of the film. His statement is that the anatomical differences leave us "with an impossible costume to construct…"

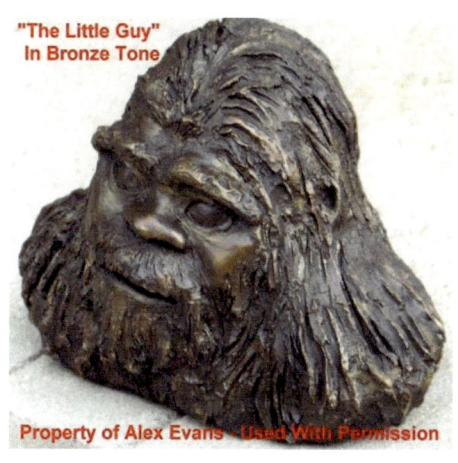

Mr. Munns stated, "The subject in the film has anatomical proportions that are very odd to say the least. Conventional creative costume design and tricks or illusions for altering regular human proportions do not achieve the result easily or effectively. Now, there are many ignorant people who have no knowledge of designing or fabricating creature costumes (that) will try to tell you differently because, in their ignorance, they fail to understand the difference between what is theoretically possible and what factually practical to accomplish. The simple reality is that… the human female shown could not be dressed up in any fur costume and make a perfect functioning performance equal to the Patterson-Gimlin subject performance.

The challenge of putting a human into a fur costume to fake the PGF is far more difficult and questionable than the hoax believers claim that it is."

In short, Mr. Munns stated that "You cannot alter where the knees or elbows bend. She has long upper leg and short lower leg." Due to the structure of the creature in the film, "If you could find a suit to match all the criteria necessary (a suit other experts have testified was not possible in 1967), you could not find a human who could wear that suit."

Arm Length Vs. Leg Length (Intermembral Index IM):

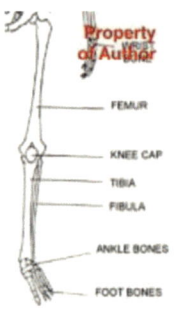

Dr. Jeff Meldrum, Paleontologist, Idaho State University has taught a ratio known as the Intermembral Index or IM. Basically, the IM is the ratio of the arm length to the leg length of a subject times one hundred (to remove the decimal). In Humans this IM ratio is 72.

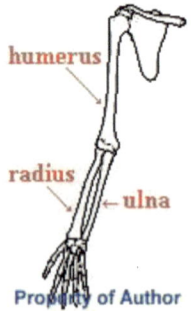

In 1998, the British Broadcasting Company, BBC, approved and financed a program for their network to "disprove" the Patterson Gimlin Film by creating a state of the art costume and putting a man inside to

prove that it could be done without a having to have done it. It is true that this project was being done over thirty years after the original film came into being. This new
film would be taking advantage of all the latest technology available, with no regard as to its availability in 1967. They theorized that the people who made us believe in Wookies and Ewoks, Apes that ruled planets and all such creations would surely debunk the claim that the suit used in that long ago film was impossible to duplicate in these conditions. This is that suit:

There are two major differences in the red suit with the man inside and the picture of Patty that are readily evident. First, pay close attention to the head and shoulder positions in the turn to look back. Patty's head sits very low on her shoulders. Her neck is very short so that when she turns, her chin goes into her shoulder, preventing it from rotating further to the rear. The result is that the shoulder has to be rotated back and out of the way for her to swivel her head far enough to effect the "look back" seen in frame 352 of the film. In the red suited figure, this is not a problem as the head sits high atop the pedestal that is the neck and can swivel over the top of the shoulder as it is shown doing here. The difference is quite obvious. The second obvious anomaly is created by the difference in the length of the arms. In that same red suited figure the right arm is in approximately the same position as its swing ends above the hip. That individual's hand is above the level of his buttocks. Compare that to the length and position of Patty's arm and hand. Her arms end well below her buttocks, not above as in the red suited figure.

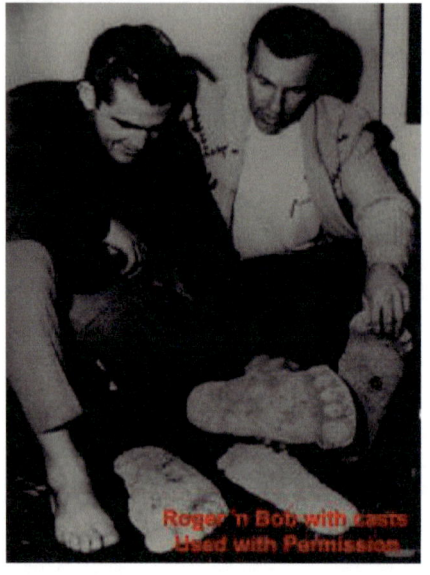

Once again, as in all such endeavors, not only was the Patterson-Gimlin film not disproved, but, in essence, it served to offer very good evidence for the veracity of that film. Aside from the fact that the person in suit could not begin to duplicate the compliant gait of the actual Sasquatch, a mere glance shows a very glaring error. Please note the relative arm lengths in the two figures. The red suited fake has arms that, in relation to the size of its body are HUMAN in form. The black figure, Patty, from the film frame 352, has arms that are much longer in relationship to her body. In fact, BBC, after airing this show issued a disclaimer stating that the data contained therein did not refute the claims of the Patterson-Gimlin Film.

Intermembral Index

Dr. Meldrum describes the Intermembral Index as the ratio of the arm as measured from the shoulder to the wrist, to the leg, measured from the hip to the ankle times one hundred. The one hundred factor is simply to clear the decimal from the result. Mathematically, that is Arm Length divided by Leg Length times one hundred or: AL / LL X 100

In primate species, all members have a distinct and specific IM. They break down as follows:

In a human, the IM is 72

In a chimpanzee, the IM is 108

In a gorilla, the IM is 122

In a sasquatch, the IM is 84

As can be readily seen here, the IM of human and sasquatch are remarkably similar but certainly not identical. It is this difference that an be used to make qualitative evaluations on reported sasquatch photographs and videos.

Typical Arm Extender

If we return to frame 72 of the Patterson Gimlin Film again, the arm length and the leg length are readily apparent and can be easily measured. Also, the arm and the leg are at the same distance from the lens in the same plane so no distortion to foreshortening is introduced into the exercise. The previously discussed calculation using the formula provided by Dr. Meldrum yields an IM of this figure to be 84. That measurement and calculation places it firmly into the range expected from its species.

At this point the ardent skeptic, the sort that this booklet is designed for would state something like, "Oh they just used an arm extender to make it correct…" Let us examine this more closely.

I measured my arm as best as I could in doing it alone and came up with the following data: Arm Length = 25"… Leg Length = 34.5"… therefore, my IM is 25/34.5X100=72.4… While this places me most firmly as human in structure, it creates a problem for he who would use an arm extender to achieve an IM of 84 as evidenced by the figure in the film. Solving the equation to yield a known IM is as follows:

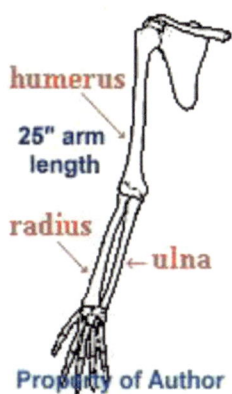

(AL / 34.5) X 100 = 84 or, **AL = 84 X 34.5 / 100 = 29**

This means, simply stated that my arm length of twenty five inches would have to be extended by four inches to achieve the desired result. In viewing the figure here, where would that four inches be added? If it were done as in the figure above, that would make the lower arm well out of proportion to the upper arm. In Frame 72, it is very evident that the elbow is exactly where it should be placed in the arm. As has been stated prior: "The elbow cannot be relocated." It simply is where it is.

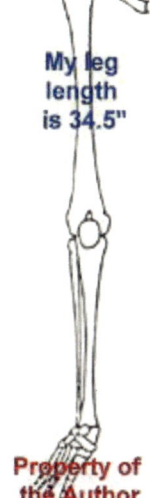

A common ploy to trick the eye is to use oversized hands in the form of huge gloves to convey the idea of a longer arm. There was a recent video released by a fellow attempting to "disprove" the film... used this ploy, but the result was so emphatically terrible, it is beyond reason to ever believe it could be even remotely possible. Look at the hands in the film and it is readily apparent that they are in proportion to the rest of the body, not some outsized grotesqueness perpetrated by one who would have us believe his tripe.

There is one other method for achieving the desired ratio. Perhaps one could reduce my leg length to the requisite twenty nine inches by somehow removing five and a half inches from its present length. Somehow, I think that might be even more objectionable to me than the process of adding the needed length to my arms. In short, there is really no feasible way short of surgery to alter this Intermembral Index formula or measuring criteria.

Know Your Players

Knowing your players is a very important concept in dealing with things pertaining to the veracity of any subject. It is especially pertinent here. Do any of the skeptics denying the truth of this film know any of the persons they quote? Do they know that individual's propensity for truth vs. lies? Do they know what this person stands for in life? Have they had experience in business with them? What are the "fruits on their trees?" If they were accused in a court of law of being open-minded, would there be enough evidence to convict them? Do they know their players?

I KNOW Bob Gimlin personally and a nicer, more honest, more plainly humble gentleman has never existed. Scott Sandsberry, a reporter for the Yakima Herald newspaper recently completed a six-part series on the sasquatch people. In that series, he concluded with an assessment of Bob Gimlin's character. I would like to share that here:

"Gimlin's version of what happened that day, though, has never changed. And he has had plenty of incentive to change it.

Documentary filmmaker Doug Hajicek was working on a television show called 'Mysterious Encounters' more than a decade ago when, while talking to Bob Gimlin for one of the episodes, happened to (have) called the show's producers. When he mentioned he was sitting with Gimlin, Hajicek said, the producers told him to offer Gimlin $1 million to tell how he and Patterson faked the footage.

'It was instant. He didn't even have to think about it,' Hajicek said. 'I wasn't floored by it. I'd gotten to know Bob and he's just such a man of character. He doesn't lie.'

He said, 'Well, that's nice, and I'd like to take your money, but this is what happened: We came around this bend ...'"

That is Bob Gimlin. The man will look you straight in the when he tells you what happened that day. He does not equivocate; he does not stammer or stutter. He tells you what happened and, as he told me, "There were three people in that crick bottom that day, Thom. There was Roger, there was me and there was that creature. There was no one else. There was nobody named Bob Heronimous." That's good enough for me!

Conclusions on the Patterson-Gimlin Film:

Each of the experts cited in this section arrived at an independent conclusion and we shall look those now.

Analysis of the herniated quadriceps muscle by Dr. Andrew Nelson and John Chambers led them to conclude that the <u>creature in the film is NOT a fake or a hoax.</u>

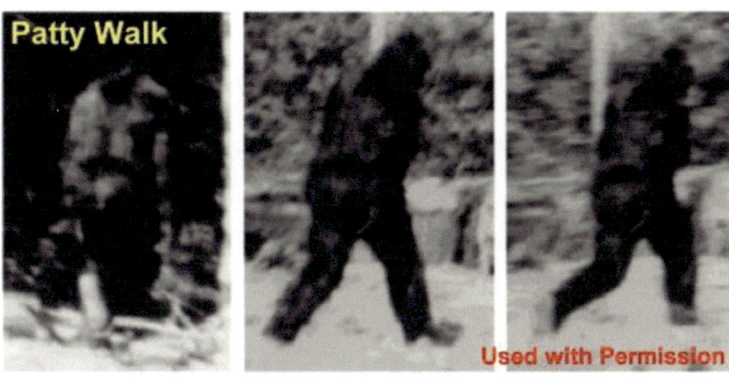

Analysis of the size of the being in the film and the compliant gait of that subject by Professor Jeffrey Meldrum, Doctor Scott Lind, Designer and Creator Bill Munns, Designer Rueben Steindorf and Designer Joe Russo led them to conclude that <u>the being in the film is of a height between 7'3" and 7'10" tall and that it walks with a gait that cannot be exactly duplicated by even an athlete.</u>

Analysis of the costume itself by Peter Brooke, Bill Munns and John

Chambers, all very well known in the costuming world and all award winners for their work, concluded that the materials needed to produce an effective costume of the type that would be necessary for that film were not available in the 1960s and even if they had been, no human could have physically been able to fill it and perform in it.

Applying Doctor Jeffrey Meldrum's Intermembral Index analysis to the figure in the film reveals an IM of 84, not the 72 found in humans nor the 108 or 122 found in chimpanzees and gorillas. 84 is the IM of Sasquatch.

It is VERY important to note here that if only ONE of the FOUR facts attested to her are true, then the figure in the film cannot be a man in a suit. That all four are attested to by qualified experts in their field yields extremely strong evidence of the veracity of the hypothesis that she is, indeed, a REAL SASQUATCH and not a man in a fur suit.

Chapter III

Footprints

Doctor Jeffrey Meldrum is, without a doubt the most knowledgeable authority on tracks and trackways of the creature we know as Sasquatch. Professor Meldrum has in his possession the largest catalog of track casts from a large, bipedal primate made all across North America. This library consists of well over two hundred casts of tracks of all sizes.

Author with track cast
Property of the Author

Professor Meldrum has stated, on one of his many appearances on "Monster Quest" or one of the other History, Discovery, or National Geographic Channel appearances, that it is not necessary to have a physical body to prove that a species exists when the preponderance of evidence so indicates. I would assume that this body of evidence needed to create this "preponderance" in the case of sasquatch would have to be enormous, indeed.

Jimmy Chilcutt
Used with Permission

The most important feature found on the best of castings are Dermal Ridges. These are the "Fingerprints", the lines on the skin that make each track individual and distinct. Research done by Mr. Jimmy Chilcutt, a forensic print examiner out of Texas has shown that the ridges on human prints are horizontal to the long axis of the foot while the ridges on the apes are diagonal to the long axis of the foot and the ridges on sasquatch are vertical to the long axis of the foot.

An extremely important aspect of examining a trackway in the wild is to know that there are changes

in the shape and position of individual toes, etc. from track to track

Recently, on one of the Discovery Channel shows devoted to the subject of the veracity of the Patterson-Gimlin Flim, Professor Began issued one of the most patently foolish statements ever made publically by a supposedly learned man. In a discussion of the footprint casts from the film, he stated that he had examined them and had concluded they were hoaxes because they were different. "They should be," he reasoned falsely, "exactly the same if they were made by the same creature as these were purported to have been."

EXCUSE ME? Has this man never tracked anything, anywhere? Of course they would not be the same! The medium the tracks are in changes. Their foot strike changes. There are so many variables that change in the matter of inches on the ground that the surest way to arouse a tracker's doubt is for the tracks to appear identical. I'm sure, by Dr. Began's rationale, he'd be quite happy with the trackway to the right in the above illustration while the trackway to the left shows continuous differentiation from track to track... as it should in a normal trackway.

This differentiation indicates motion of the toes, suggesting that the subject is flesh and blood and not merely a rigid material used to fake the footprints.

In the London Trackway, discovered in February of 2012 near the Oregon town of Cottage Grove, a series of over one hundred and twenty footprints in one trackway were found and cast in plaster. In those tracks, some showed all five toes and others showed only four. Evidently the author of these tracks in walking across the muddy lakebed was sometimes holding his small toe up from the ground and, at other times, placing it on the ground. The result was a variation in prints from one to the next in violation of Dr. Began's statement... his false statement.

Jimmy Chilcutt, forensic print examiner stated: "My testimony puts people in jail, so it is important that I be complete and accurate in my examinations of (dermal ridges in) prints."

Mr. Chilcutt has studied the prints of all the great apes as well as the sasquatch prints found and has verified the facts stated above as to the orientation of the lines of the ridges.

Doctor Henner Fahrenbach of the Oregon Regional Primate Research Center hypothesized that any population of tracks should have a natural distribution of sizes, widths and areas as would any animal species, including the human species. Using data he garnered from Dr.  Meldrum's extensive library of foot castings along with hundreds of other verified castings from various sources spanning over one hundred years and

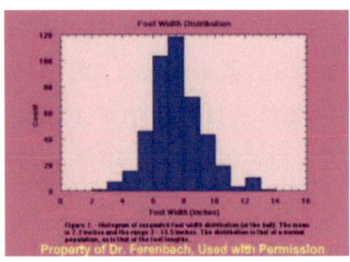
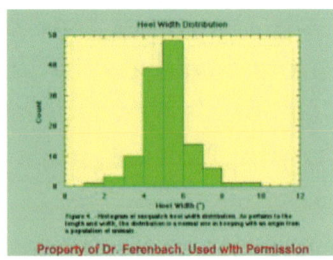
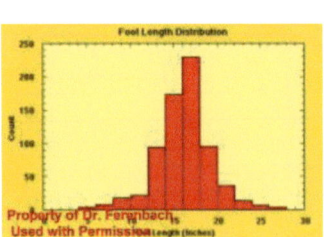
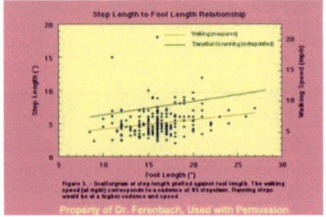

geographically spanning North America, he created a histogram of the data accumulated.

As can be seen from the graphs shown, Dr. Fahrenbach has demonstrated that the raw histograms yield in analysis to standard Bell Shaped Curves indicating that across centuries and a continent, the data comes from a living population rather than being faked.

An Observation:

Grayback Mtn Trackway

After closely examining these trackways, I find one thing in common to them all. There are NO marks near them that might have come from a person creating them to perpetrate a hoax. There are some scuff marks in the Sierra Trackway that were made by the discoverer in photographing the tracks prior to making plaster casts but this does not constitute a way to have manufactured the trackway.

How would you create such a trackway without leaving telltale marks of having done so? Stilts? With a Midtarsal Break and a step of more than four feet? On Snow? In a wilderness? What do you think? Two of these were discovered at over ten thousand feet elevation in the Sierra Nevada Mountains. In fact, Mr. Avalos has a standing reward of $10,000 to the maker of the trackway he studied here if they can come forth and show him how it was made.

Conclusions:

Jimmy Chicutt stated after his investigations: "There is Sasquatch (Species) living in North America. The prints (I have investigated) are neither human nor are they Ape."

Dr. Henner Fahrenbach stated after his analysis of the statistical data: "In all likelihood, there is a large primate walking about in North American forests."

Dr. Jeff Meldrum stated that: "My personal collection of over two hundred footprint casts suggest that there is a large, bipedal primate in North America."

Chapter IV
DNA Evidence

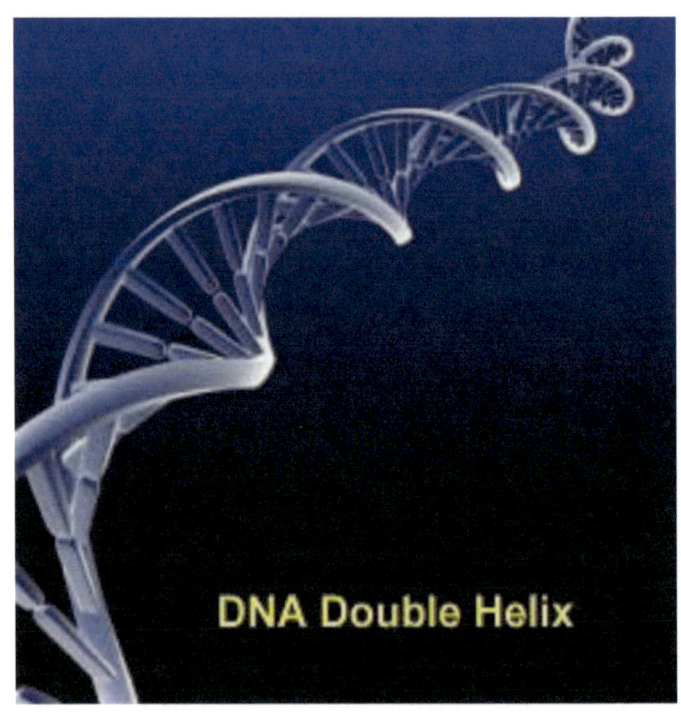

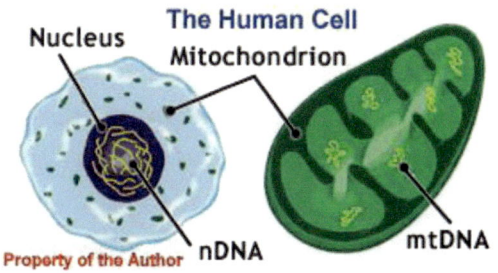

DNA is probably one of the least understood and most misrepresented facet of sasquatch research. DNA does not "PROVE" the existence of anything. It is a statistical database that, when a specimen sample is compared to the base, it can be identified… provided the DNA being compared has a match in the database. Any DNA found and identified from an unknown, or heretofore unknown and unidentified species will simply come back as "Unknown Primate"

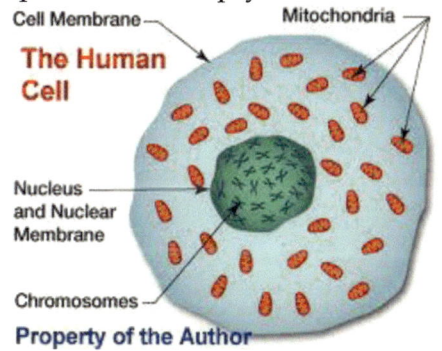

There are two major sources of DNA in the cell. The more common source, the Mitochondrial DNA or mtDNA is found, as the name would suggest, in the Mitochondria of the cell. The accompanying figure shows the orientation, in two dimensions of the location of the Mitochondria in the cell outside the nucleus. There are many Mitochondria per cell and all contain mtDNA strands within their structure. The second, or Nuclear DNA is contained within the nucleus of the cell and is contained on the forty three pairs of chromosomes in that nucleus. Of those pairs, one side comes from our mother and the other side comes from our father, combining to create a new genetic assembly in each individual.

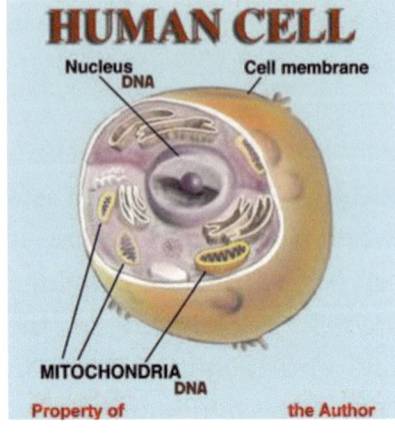

The mtDNA comes to us from our female progenitors... from the female side of the mating. It is the signature provided to us by our matrilineal line... mother, grandmother, great grandmother and et cetera. From this material, it is possible to identify our most ancient grandmothers as far back as our early beginnings. This mtDNA is by far the easier to obtain from samples gathered from parts of entire creatures. It is not subject to deterioration as rapidly as Nuclear DNA. There are many more Mitochondria in the cells

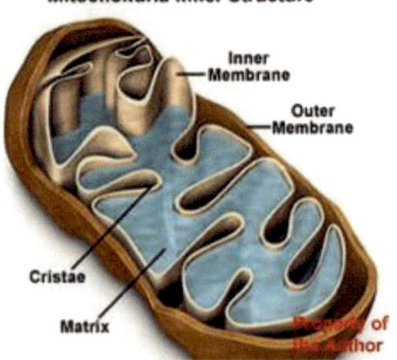

than there are chromosomes in the nucleus of that cell, so the very odds of DNA found heavily favors the fact of it being of the mtDNA variety. It is also the less likely to be corrupted so is more viable for a longer period of time. In some organs or systems such as hair, it is like to be the only DNA found.

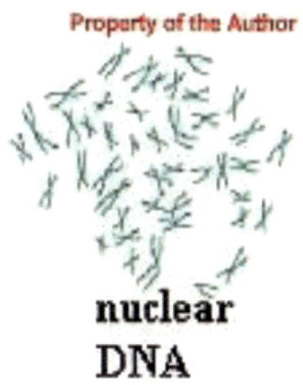

nuclear DNA

Nuclear DNA is not limited to just the female markers as is the mtDNA. As such, it can show the genealogy of the male side of the mating as well as the female. Mapping of the nDNA is involved and can be very time consuming but the data gleaned can be of most profound value.

Dr. Melba Ketchum
Used with Permission

Today, as of this writing, there are two major DNA studies in progress. The first, "The Sasquatch Genome Project" headed by Dr. Melba Ketchum of DNA Diagnostics, Palestine, TX is nearing publication after having been subjected to the most rigorous peer review possible. While it is premature to discuss the findings of this study that took advantage of over a hundred samples from across North America and is coauthored by several of the premier names in DNA diagnostics in the United States the results are spectacular and, as Dr. Ketchum once said, "I've got the goods!" Personally, I am waiting with bated breath for the publication of this report.

The second major study of this genre has just been announced and a call for samples has been issued by Oxford University in Oxford, England. The Sykes Study will collect samples from around the world and may complement the Sasquatch Genome Project and could answer relationship questions between the various species and subspecies of these beings from around the world. Be it the Yeren from China, the Almastie from Russia or the Yeti from the Himalayas, connections will be known and documented.

As far-reaching as the Ketchum Report and the Sykes report are to science and to the beings themselves, they are not the first DNA studies conducted on sasquatch. There are, to my knowledge, two major studies that were conducted prior to the Sasquatch Genome Project.

A few years ago, Dr. Craig Newton of B.C. Research in Vancouver, British Columbia, Canada was provided hairs from the Skookum cast taken in south-central Washington state. Dr. Newton attempted to analyze the DNA from these hairs and found it to be human in structure. As a result, he dismissed his testing by stating that the sample had to have been contaminated with the DNA of those gathering the sample.

It is important to note here that, for some as to now unknown reason, it is very, very difficult to extract DNA from sasquatch hair. Dr. Ketchum, in relating this to me, stated that what made this most unusual was the fact that in most animals, hair shafts yield DNA quite readily. She went on to say that the DNA extracted after major difficulty was, invariably, mtDNA, meaning it came from the matrilineal side. Matrilineal or mtDNA is going to be pure human in sasquatch.

I spoke to members of the team that worked with that cast, including Mr. Richard Noll and Dr. Jeff Meldrum about the methods used and was assured that great care was taken to ensure that no contamination occurred in the gathering phase. I am also quite sure that Dr. Newton's lab would never contaminate any sample left in their care. I am left, therefore, with the conclusion that Dr. Newton found and proved precisely what was there but the science of sasquatch DNA being in its infancy, he simply did not realize what he had. I'm sure if he'd had DNA for testing other than from hair shafts, he would have seen the facts as they actually were.

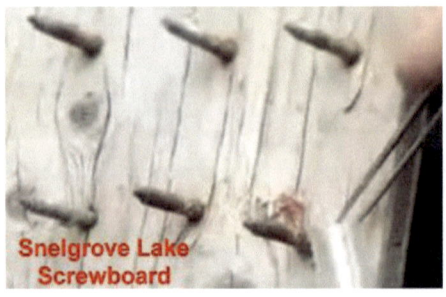

In 2009, Dr. Jeff Meldrum and Microbiologist, Dr. Kurt Nelson of the University of Minnesota journeyed to a remote cabin in upper Ontario, Canada on Snelgrove Lake. At that cabin there was found a screw board that had been stepped upon by something with an approximately eighteen inch long foot, leaving a quantity of dried blood on the board. Dr. Nelson was able to isolate DNA that from the blood that varied by only one marker from that of human DNA. That one marker was one of the five markers that differ from humans in chimpanzees, our formerly closest relative. Dr. Nelson determined that the DNA he extracted was 99.4% to 99.6% identical to human DNA. Comparison in this manner shows chimpanzee DNA to be 98.3% the same as human DNA.

DNA Conclusions:

Dr. Craig Newton, prematurely, I think, dismissed his results considering the facts that have surfaced later in this area of study.

Dr. Kurt Nelson is convinced he has isolated DNA from our closest relative as a species.

Dr. Melba Ketchum is poised to rock the scientific world with her impending release of a peer reviewed report that will link us enexorably to a heretofore unknown species.

Conclusion:

I will conclude this treatise with a statement from a well known and oft quoted, Dr. D. Jeffrey Meldrum, Associate Professor of Paleontology, Idaho State University, Pocatello, Idaho:

"I have weighed and considered the evidence... I have now reached a point that is seems more incredible that all of this (the century long series of sightings, tracks, etc.) is a series of spurious hoaxing spanning decades if not centuries than it is to entertain the likelihood that a new species of high order primate may exist and may soon join the family of the ranks of primates..."

To this I can only add, amen... let it be.

For Further Study

Documentaries:
Monster Quest Discovery Channel – Snelgrove Lake Monster Quest Discovery Channel – Critical Evidence
Monster Quest Discovery Channel – Legend of the Hairy Beast
Monster Quest Discovery Channel – Mysterious Ape Island
Monster Quest Discovery Channel – Sierra Sasquatch
National Geographic Channel – Sasquatch, Legend Meets Science
Bill Munns youtube analysis:
:http://www.youtube.com/watch?v=MKUwdHex1Zs
http://www.youtube.com/watch?v=V9WO8c38cRo
21 Degrees of Difference:
http://www.youtube.com/watch?v=SRi1VLBxtZc

Books:

The Locals	Thom Powell
Enoch	Autumn Williams
Valley of the Skookum	Sali Sheppard Wolford
Where Bigfoot Walks	Robert M. Pyle
Visits of the Forest People	Julie Scott
The Discovery of the Sasquatch	John Bindernagel
Know The Sasquatch/Bigfoot	Christopher L. Murphy
Raincoast Sasquatch	J. Robert Alley
Tribal Bigfoot	David Paulides
Impossible Visits	Christopher Noel
Voices in the Wilderness	Ron Morehead
Ghosts of Ruby Ridge	Thom Cantrall
Tracking Bigfoot	Lori Simmons

Made in United States
Troutdale, OR
11/18/2023